This page is intentionaly left blank.

© 2020 HRM Incorporated — Publishing Div.

**Tin Man: Introspection of A Beating Heart**

All rights reserved. No part of this publication may be reproduced, stored in a retrieval system or transmitted in any form or by any means, electronic, mechanical, photocopying, recording or otherwise without the prior permission of the publisher or in accordance with the provisions of the Copyright, Designs and Patents Act 1988 or under the terms of any license permitting limited copying issued by the Copyright Licensing Agency.

**Published by:** HRM Incorporated — Publishing Div.

**Editor:** K.A. Bryan

**Illustrations By:** J Marcus

**Cover Design by:** J Marcus and A.C. Bryan

**ISBN-13:** 978-0-9908788-9-6

# Tin Man: Introspection of A Beating Heart
Aurielle Chelayne

# Tin Man: Introspection of A Beating Heart

AURIELLE CHELAYNE

# TABLE OF CONTENTS

## ACKNOWLEDGEMENTS

To The Ones.................................................................................13

## IN YOUTH

Heart(less) ..................................................................................17
Just Enough.................................................................................20
The Garden..................................................................................21
A Rose .........................................................................................22
A Thorn........................................................................................24
Patiently......................................................................................25
Trauma: The Cycle......................................................................26
The Mask ....................................................................................28
Dollface.......................................................................................30
We're Not Okay............................................................................31

## IN LOVE

Beautiful Envy ............................................................................35
Tin Man's Lament........................................................................36
A Kiss ..........................................................................................37
Beauty.........................................................................................38
Lovely .........................................................................................41
The Tempest of a Union ..............................................................44
Wonderland.................................................................................45
To Have Loved ............................................................................47

| | |
|---|---|
| To Have Known | 48 |
| Smudges | 51 |
| Illusions | 52 |
| Ghost of You | 53 |
| A Heart In Mending | 55 |

# IN ISOLATION

| | |
|---|---|
| The Witch | 59 |
| The End | 62 |
| The Jester | 64 |
| Isolation | 65 |

# IN MADNESS

| | |
|---|---|
| The Creation | 69 |
| Chaos Brew | 70 |
| The Monster | 71 |
| The Favorite | 72 |
| Stoic | 74 |
| Potential of A Rose | 77 |
| Secret | 78 |
| Overtone | 79 |
| Stay | 81 |
| In Silence | 82 |
| The Madness: An Obsession | 83 |
| Ophelia's Song | 84 |
| Lies | 85 |

# IN FREEDOM

| | |
|---|---|
| Scarecrow | 89 |
| My Joy Was Buried | 90 |
| A Moment | 92 |
| Hope In A Wasteland | 93 |

| | |
|---|---|
| Beauty Reborn | 94 |
| An Aria | 96 |
| A Thousand | 97 |
| Hope | 99 |
| Joy | 100 |
| A Bird | 101 |
| Lionheart | 103 |

# ACKNOWLEDGEMENTS

To My Parents and Brothers,

Your constant presence has helped shaped me into who I am today; I love you all.

Tin Man

# TO THE ONES

To the one who sits alone, wondering when someone will notice you;
to the one whose pain seems to grow with each passing day;
to the one who has so much to say, but the words come out jumbled;
to the one who has tasted failure, and is uncertain of how to move forward;
to the one whose cries have gone unheard for so long;
to the one who is a constant target for cruel words and crueler actions;
to the one who has big dreams, and no clear idea of how to make it happen;
to the one who from much has been taken, but little has been given.

This is for you.
Take courage, dear one.

Hardships pass, and soon you'll find yourself in a place you never thought you'd quite get to. I hope that one day, you'll realize each little step you struggled to take has brought you farther than you ever thought you could go; that you'll realize, the weight you used to carry has become lighter- that you've become freer. I hope that one day- in the future- when you read this, you'll be proud of the work you've done and the person you've become; that you'll realize one day, that your heart is no longer in mending. Instead, it will be healed.

This, my friend, is for you.

# IN YOUTH

Tin Man
# HEART(LESS)

"Stay away from me!" you scream,
My soul reams, from all your insecurities.
You call me some kind of freak, I'm weak
From all the lies that you've told of me.

How am I supposed to move on?
All my hope is gone.
I'm no longer new,
All that's left is my heart's residue.

                                          You push me to break me,
                                            You pull me to shake me;
                                          You crush me to make me
                                              Believe that you hate me.

For                                              so                                            long

                    I believed that your arms—
the "would-be" warmth against all of life's storms;
    The protection against the dead of night,
      A beacon to keep hope within sight.

If that's it, I'll make a hasty retreat;
There must be some other refuge to seek.
Your bitterness unfolds,
as the story's told;
While I begin to make
my own solitary abode.

I build me walls made of stone;
Never again will I leave this comfort zone.
If this is what it means to be loved
Then I've had more than enough.

Brick,
        by brick,
                by brick,

I've become used to being desolate –
A wasteland, barren of any emotion,
Giving Numbness all my devotion.

## Tin Man

I've spent years here,
        in my emotion torn tower,
                Only having to rely on my own power;

I've constantly been told what I feel doesn't matter,
I've lived alone, so what's left of my heart won't shatter.

                              But that wasn't enough no, it's true;
                Because life gave me lemons and you know what lemons do-
                      They sting and burn until there's nothing left,
                            Same goes for my heart-

        no, the hole in my chest.

# JUST ENOUGH

Just below
the
surface
bubbles
an emotion
most curious.
Pacing,
feet-worn holes in a mental carpet
begging for help –
unheard.
Doors closed, air-tight
lips sealed
silence pushing against words that need to be said.
"I need, I need, I need,"
your mantra repeated
over tenuous years.
"What about me?"
A question given voice
only in my head
to hollowed walls,
moving only the slightest
cobweb.
How many times
have I
let the emotion
sizzle
just enough
not to
blow up?

Tin Man
# THE GARDEN

This morning
I rose
to find you
walking
in the garden
looking – seeking
wandering a path, lost in motion
your heart,
innocent
barely standing
on wobbly legs
newly searching
for wonders – uninhibited;

But
I
was in search
of you
before stars
knew
their names
and
before light
filled
all darkness
–
I knew
you.

# A ROSE

A rose
Silent, beautiful, lonely;
Caged in glass- on display.
Timeless in all its symbol;
yet subject to life's hourglass.
Petal by petal,
withers and decays- singularly-
on a stage so tragic.


A girl
Lonely, ridiculed, lovely;
Caged in pearls- on display.
Ruby lips, her sign of elegance;
framed by haunted, tired eyes.
Moment by moment,
She withers under their words - singularly-
a jester for their enjoyment.


A rose, a girl
Isolated, yet alluring;
Caged together in melancholy.
Voiceless, but beautiful.

Tin Man

# A THORN

You blame me
for the blood on your hands,
when you were the one
to squeeze me tight –
a mighty grip
        never quite loosened.

You blame me
when I do not conform
to the stem;
Pricking at
your fraying nerves
once again –
an iron hand
        desperate to control.

I am a thorn,
you desperately abhor;
the stain of your weakened dominance.

The thorn of a stem,
never quite fitting in;
the lone sign of imperfection.

Tin Man
# PATIENTLY

Standing
on the sidelines,
praised, but never chosen
waiting patiently
for a chance –
a moment
to preen under
your sparse attention
wondering
when you would notice
me.

Long has the sun
sunk below
an eternal horizon,
billowy pink skies
melted into
rich indigo;
Yet I still
wait
for you
to choose me –
patiently.

# TRAUMA: THE CYCLE

You wondered what it is like
to experience a trauma not your own?
You marvel at how inspiring
overcoming these atrocious hangers-on could be;
Expecting a beautiful story of intrigue and ingenuity.

                        You wonder, so I will tell you.

My grandfather's trauma roars loud with a rage most foul,
culminating in a heady mix of alcohol and depression;
Passed down as a mantle to the unsuspecting son
of muddied bloodlines and familial secrets –
shoddily strapped together by detrimental promises.

                        This is his unspoken inheritance.

My father, unsuspectingly born into the cruel embrace
of loss and confusion,
Small fists tightly wrapped around feeble ones;
Transferring of agony celebrated by a desperate cry.

My father's trauma, not so easily seen, simmers low and boils hot;
Pulled to and fro, trying to sort through
generations of unresolved emotional turbulence –
Fighting fiercely against the ancestral yoke forced around his neck.

Is this to be the generational wealth
        that awaits the sons of my father?

## Tin Man

Yet...

First born, not male-born,
A girl in the place where kings are meant to be.
So tell me, who will carry my trauma?

Will my daughter, back sweating, still till a barren ground?
Will her daughter, voice stilted, still carry an ever-increasing yoke around her neck?
Who will bear the weight of it?

Will they still claw at taped mouths,
nails bleeding;
Muffled voices shouting to be heard?
Will they still be offered up on social butcher blocks-
sacrifice for a blinded people?
Will their lives be spectacle, never human?

The bones of my father have been hung for all to see;
Every bleeding ligament placed on top a decadent mantle.
You are curious, I know,
of what pain he'd been made to endure
as his trauma clung to painted frames
garnering crowds who gawk
at the chains and scars –
delighting in the story they do not bear the weight of.

We are but canvas stretched o'er generations of ill-fitted wood;
painted by our silence,
Showcasing scars handcarved by the generations before,
sold to the masses.

       Tell me, how much have you paid for my trauma?

# THE MASK

She thought about quitting- quite a lot actually. Not just quitting a job, or school, or whatever else people usually talk about quitting; she thinks about quitting...everything. Sometimes quitting seems so appealing. The idea of completely letting go- of just laying down and giving up. After all of the feelings of frustrations, feelings of failure, and just utter fatigue.

She was tired. So, so tired... and theoretically she shouldn't be. She was still young; she hadn't really had a chance to experience life yet... not since she was given that mask.

Yet the mounting pressure that everyone put on her against her parents' wishes... She was the 'model child,' the 'best example,' the one that parents ushered their kids to and pointed at as the epitome of what a kid should be; but to her she was just a zoo animal- a performance monkey meant to dance and sing and clap when the adults asked. Yet these adults didn't understand that when their backs were turned, when they pushed their kids- her peers- off on her, she was isolated. They didn't understand the visciousness she was greeted with- the vitriol. They were content to turn a blind eye to the ongoing stress the girl was put under.

So, of course she was tired.

Everyone assumed she had it all together- that she would never break. And for a while, they were right. Each day, she painfully donned the mask that they were comfortable with- big eyes, bright smile, laugh on cue, "yes, ma'am," do your homework, get on honor roll, do well in dance practice, audition for theater, "be a good example."

## Tin Man

The signs were so easy to spot, yet so few took notice. Those big eyes became surrounded by bags, her bright smiled had waned to the point of being strained, her laughter had become stilted or would catch in her throat, her "yes ma'am" had become just "yes," her homework was done mindlessly, it became harder for her to remember simple dates, dancing became harder, and theater began to give her anxiety. The carefully crafted mask she wore, was cracking.

She briefly thought that she should figure out a way to fix the mask;
                                                        (she was used to it.)
but that proved to be more work than she thought.
                (she hadn't realized just how weak the mask had become.)
It wasn't until she realized that some pieces of her mask (that she tried to glue back in place) no longer fit together, that she tried wandering out into the world without it.

At first, she thought it terrifying; but soon, she realized that the weight she had been carrying– the responsibility that had been thrust upon her by errant adults– had crumbled right in front of her eyes.

Those first few breaths were a shock– everything was so different than they had been previously. The next few breaths, she savored– she hadn't had freedom like this before; the freedom to learn and grow like kids her own age. When she realized this, her eyes, once dull, began to take on a new light; her smile, once waning, became bright; her laughter become joyful and hearty.

When she finally decided to let go of the mask, she realized she had found her true self.

# DOLLFACE

Your color, on the surface
Nobody wants to purchase
Your hair will be the scare
Of a lifetime don't you dare
Your waist is not in place
There's no beauty in your face
Even with plastic in your fate
You'll never sell, Dollface

Your eyes are like the marsh
And your voice is much too harsh
Your skin is so unclear
Have you even looked in the mirror?
Just try to comprehend
With those girls you don't contend
Don't try to win the race
It won't end well, Dollface

Tell me, how much did it cost you
to destroy a child's point of view?
Does it amuse you
to destroy others like the world destroyed you?

Tin Man
# WE'RE NOT OKAY

Tell me, tell me
have you seen Johnny?
Have you seen him, he's really quite charming.
                          We were supposed to meet here,
                             in this much-too-full house;
                          we'd hang with all our friends,
                                drink a little,
                               then we'd bounce.
        But ever since I entered,
the music's drowned out all our words;
      yet the look on people's faces
speaks more than anything I've heard.

(There's one less soul at this party).

          Now I can
            feel
         the alcohol
           pulsing,
        through my veins
      But hasn't made the
          looming
       sadness go away
   Houston, the lonliness
    has quickly begun
       to escalate
I don't know why but
        we are
         not
     doing okay.

# IN LOVE

Tin Man
# BEAUTIFUL ENVY

the wind gently
caresses
the leaves of the
-
tree
shaking loose
its splendor
petals effortlessly
glide
in an aimless
fashion
-
draped upon
your crown
the sun
nuzzling
your skin in
reverance
kissing
your brow
-
never have I
been more
envious
of a petal

# TIN MAN'S LAMENT

oh no,
I'm missing
a heart;
ice cold,
I'm trying to stop
–
the bleeding.
at first
it came
as a shock
since you
were the only one
I thought I could
trust.

it's fine
I'm used to
the pain;
since no one's ever
asked me
how I got
this way.
believe me
if only I had
known
that you have
a habit of
dealing the
killing blow.

Tin Man

# A KISS

A kiss to the
-
temple
is worse
than a bullet,
when the mouth
those lips belong to
have become a constant
-
menace.

With a vengeance
roaring loud
your words cut deep
-
bleeding me.

Why am I
the only
casualty
in our war of
-
words?

# BEAUTY

"Beauty."

You call the name;
golden locks wispy,
bouncing in the wind -
reflecting sunlight.
Happiness radiating
from the very essence of the name.

>                                    But my hair is not golden.

"Beauty."

You say the name-
        prayerfully, reverently.
Ruby lips painted to perfection,
framing a sweet smile;
skin milky and smooth.

>                      But my skin is a muddy mixture of sand and toffee.

Tin Man

"Beauty."

You caress the name-
        anxious and unsure.
Cerulean orbs, filled with mirth
and a playfulness that comes with ease,
keeps you hooked-
                you are enraptured.

"Beauty."

Your voice carries with the wind.
Yet again, you've surrendered to the siren.

"Beauty."

        Your voice is loud and clear;
        Your longing palpable to my ears.

                      "Beauty."

                        That name...


                                                  "Beauty."

My eyes are not pools of blue;
My smile is unsure, but true.
My lips are not a ruby hue-
I guess I am not Beauty to you.

You, who call the name like a sacred tune;
You, who embrace the name as the stars embrace the moon.
You, who search for Beauty in one place;
You, who have never truly seen Beauty's face.

You...

Your words echo in my ears
        loud and clear-

"You are not Beauty."

I had always thought I was Beauty;

now I realize that I was Beast.

Tin Man
# LOVELY

Beauty,
isn't she a beauty?
Her waist, a template of perfection.
Truly,
she's positively stunning;
smooth skin, no blemish in sight.

What'll it take to hold your attention?
Must I intake air for my dinner?
I'm still lying awake, holding onto
Tthe hope that I'll break –
away from
the mould you have for me.

Why can't you see, that I am lovely?
I can't believe I almost let your lies ruin me.
I'll never be, your warped view of beauty;
I won't concede, take up for myself,
be the savior I need.

Trusting,
you said I was too trusting;
I saw too much good in the corrupted.
Truly,
you'd rather I be stunning;
all frills, no brain in my head.

What'll it take to hold your attention?
Must I obtain a sense of rebellion?
I'm still lying awake, holding onto
Tthe hope that I'll break –
away from
the mould you have for me.

Why can't you see, that I am lovely?
I can't believe I almost let your lies ruin me.
I'll never be, your warped view of beauty;
I won't concede, take up for myself,
be the savior I need.

# Tin Man

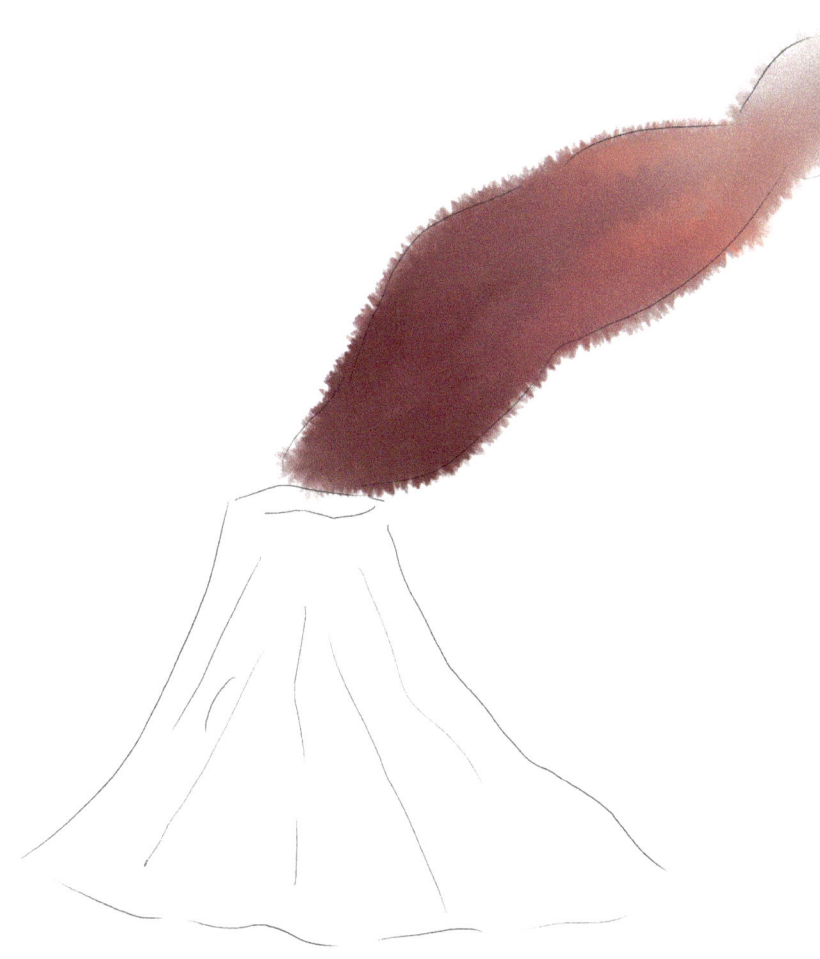

# THE TEMPEST OF A UNION

Very seldom do I sing aloud the score of my heart;
But when I do, it's to the bare walls of a mausoleum,
Where the bones held captive all listen enraptured.

                When will I make an audience of the living?
                  Who will listen to my song intently?

I am a volcano, emotions ready to burst in a moment –
An avalanche waiting to smother someone with my love.
You have deemed my tightly sewn shut lips an easy prey;
Not realizing a storm is brewing –
                                                  Barely contained.

Soon my loving vengeance will overtake your very being;
Quickly caught up in the dissonance of my heart –
I will gather you to me,
Tuck you into my embrace;
Until we emerge a harmony so sweetly attuned
                to the essence of our union.

Tin Man
# WONDERLAND

We stumbled into Wonderland.

A place so fanciful,

       so mythical,

              so ethereal;

but it was different than we imagined.

It was more decadent than we thought;
more worldly, more primal.
We were quickly swept away by our most base desires;
Indulging ourselves with every evil fruit we could hold –
gorging ourselves with every sweet vice we could see.
Eagerly, earnestly, we waded into unknown waters
with the promise that we wouldn't lose sight of the shore;

But ever so slowly,

       imperceptibly...

The Wonderland we knew, escaped us –
turned into something we didn't account for.
Something that our children's stories
and make-believe didn't warn us about.
Something that no amount of fairy dust,
no potion, no spell could emulate or control.

The light we so loved blinded us, plunging us into darkness.
        A darkness so visceral, so bitter.
        Here, the riddles of our hearts found their way into our actions.
        Here, the mirrors we so desperately tried to break,
        cut us.
        Here, we found our puzzle pieces connected–
        but they didn't make a coherent image.
        Here, the selves we tried so desperately to hide, confronted us.
        Here, all innocence we had, died.

Soon the darkness, the Madness, swallowed us whole–
Destroying whatever it could in its wake.
The aftermath, the left overs, the remnants of what we were...
        All consumed.
        All used.
        Only ashes remained.

        We stumbled into Wonderland;
                and Wonderland devoured us.

Tin Man
# TO HAVE LOVED

My dreams have led me to places I have not yet realized —
They have led me to possible realities.
We have met and loved so many times;
that I know you down to your last atom.

Your voice, your scent, the very essence of you
has found its way into my very being;
The sweetest of unions — two became one,
two halves of a whole.

Your words gripped me like the chill of autumn;
like when the impatient winter begins to make its presence known.
A chill so deep it became a part of me —
of my very bones.
I carried them with me, always, even in my sleep.
So tell me —

How am I supposed to let you go
when I feel your presence in my very soul?

# TO HAVE KNOWN

She had seen him.

For years now, he had visited her. Night after night he held her, embraced her. He listened to her worries, her frustrations, her struggles, her thoughts. He had shared in her joys, her hopes, her despair and regrets. All without offering a single word. Instead, he gave her the comforting silence she so desperately desired.

When the work days were long and arduous; when the city was much too loud and her thoughts much too crowded- he was there. When the sky unleashed its pent up fury; when the sun smiled on her face through her dirty windows- he was there. When all the things she bottled up, broke; when the only sound she could utter a sigh- he was still there.

Waiting. Ever so patiently waiting. As time moved forward, he remained. As the seasons slowly faded one after another, he was still there.

He held her hand when stars shown at their brightest, when they lay silently- in stillness- when there was only a breath between them. He elicited the concerns swelling from deep within her and tucked them into his very being- locked away. She relied on him.

She had known him.

She had memorized what his calloused hands felt like skimming over her arms. She had memorized what his lopsided smile looked like. She knew he pursed his lips when he was in deep thought.

## Tin Man

She could tell you exactly what his favorite shirt was. She could tell you what side of the bed he preferred. She knew that he enjoyed cold showers in the morning, oranges over apples, and being outdoors over staying indoors. She knew he only ate eggs over easy, that he hated his meat well-done.

She knew that he preferred walking to driving, that he loved to ride his bike on Saturday mornings- rain or shine. She knew that the little bump on the bridge of his nose was from a bad spill on a particularly dangerous trail. She knew that his whole body shook when he laughed.

She had missed him.

His smile, his strength, his support. She missed his hugs, how he cherished her. She missed...

She missed how he made her feel loved, his attentiveness. His eyes, so full of vigor, of life. His welcoming presence when she walked through the door; his cautious smile on a rough day. She missed the simple things: a hand to hold, a body to embrace, the way he said her name.

Now, those echoes haunt her. When she walks into the house there's only the sound of her feet. There's no warm presence, no smile, no embrace, no light, no life...

For a year now, he had stopped visiting. She feels his absence so much more at night. When the city is much too loud and her thoughts much too crowded. When her work days are long and arduous; when all the things that she'd bottled up, broke; when the only sound she can utter is a sigh. When the stars are at their brightest, she lays silently- in stillness- and there is so much more than a breath next to her.

The silence, now, wraps around her like a well-worn blanket. It encapsulates her, consumes her. It amplifies her concerns, causes them to spin rapidly around in her mind- locked away. There is no one else to rely on- the silence tells her.

It's in these moments that she wishes that she could rewind the clock; beg Father Time to reset the timer. These moments when the moon is at it's peak, when the air is still, when the sheets on his side of the bed are cold, when her thoughts keep her up. It's these moments that she realizes-

She still loves him...
                              and it is so hard to love someone when they are gone.

Tin Man
# SMUDGES

Did you finally
learn the meaning
of the dirt stains

        slathered on white tiles –
        muddy mess
        of an emotion long brewing?

                Tell me,
            have you seen them?

Our walls house many.
Each of us capriciously
trying to give a voice
to our inward struggles –
where innocence has been tainted.

# ILLUSIONS

Painted lips pressed to stained cheeks
Slowly swaying on the offbeat -
Never quite finding a rhytmn of their own.

Gangly limbs tightly wound around broad shoulders
restlessly pulling closer - seeking warmth,
yet never quite finding solace.

How long till she realizes
the arms wrapped around her are her own;
desperately trying to provide
a comfort she long thought out of reach.

Tin Man
# GHOST OF YOU

Tender hearts, paper skies
I need a little push to give light to the night
Cuz' all else is fading
And I'm patiently waiting
Here, for you

                                        Brittle dreams, encased in glass
                       Seems like the world is spinning too fast
                           Even when you fade, I'll still wait
                                             Here, for you

                    I see you
                  In every room
              You occupy my heart
                Please don't change
       Your ghost has never gone away
            And I want it to stay

Tainted hearts, tear stained cheeks
Sometimes anger's the push I need
Cuz' all pain is fading
And I'm patiently waiting
Here, for you

                              Lucid dreams, wait for (await) me
                                    In them your face I see
                         And even when you fade, I'll still wait
                                          Here, for you

I see you
In every room
You occupy my heart
Please don't change
Your ghost has never gone away
And I want it to stay

Your warmth is like a residue
Makes it hard to get over you
Even after you've been gone
I can still hear your heartbeat
It's like the sound is still echoing
Through the walls of my heart

I'll spend eternity, it seems
Always believing in a dream
That outruns me
Forever, I'll never escape
You left a ghost in your wake
My love, you can't shake

I see you
In every room
You occupy my heart
Please don't change
Your ghost has never gone away
And I want it to stay

Even when you fade, I'll still wait
Here, for you

Tin Man

# A HEART IN MENDING

It's funny how
a heart will
–
mend
since being
broken
time and time
–
again
it doesn't quite
heal
the way it
used to be

and even when the
pain
fades
–
away
a scar
is left in its
place
–
sutured closed
by an
emotional
necessity

# IN ISOLATION

Tin Man
# THE WITCH

Draped in black,
Your face green with envy;
Arms stretched wide
Towards the midnight sky.

>Chaos dancing,
>grey across the leaves,
>Anticipation raised
>orange in pre-emptive triumph;
>you are so sure
>that you will succeed,
>chartreuse fingers
>clenched in determination.

The flames burn blue,
My skin burns red;
"Burn the witch!"
Your admirers plead.

>Strained whispers,
>an incessant staccato to my vigilant ears;
>Your chanting a dull hum
>over your followers' frenzy.

Wickedness hangs thick–
Your eyes a devilish hue;
"Burn the witch!"
Your obsession said.

"Burn the witch!"
                              "Burn the witch!"
            "Burn the witch!"


The sky, once calm,
now screams with sadistic delight;
as you surround me,
joining the torrential mayhem –
drenching me in blackened ire,
smothering me in hazy wrath.

Now the words from your lips have seared my forehead,
like a brand, you exiled me –
pushing me to the edge,
expecting me to remain docile.
"You are an outcast, best to be forgotten;
lest you ruin all that you touch."

Yet, you didn't expect the chaos within
to summon a beast most primal–
a wounded animal intent on preservation,
with a voice that will not be silenced.

WITCH,
you called me, because I did not conform to what you wanted;
then, WITCH, I will be.

# Tin Man

# THE END

We waited for the end-
        Anticipating,
                hoping.
We waited for the other shoe to drop;
for all of our fears to manifest into
a truth we so firmly believed.
We craved the downfall-
        The continuous spiraling out of control;
                The crazed lust burning,
demolishing everything in its wake-

                                        Leaving nothing but ashes.

We were addicted to the hardships-
        Indulging,
                reveling.
Somehow believing they added value,
worth, to our tethering.
We coveted the rock bottom-
        The never ending cycle of pain and passion;
                The frenzied clawing, digging our way out
                    of the emotional cage we trapped each other in.

Tin Man

We didn't expect the simplicity-
                The calmness, stillness of those quiet nights
                   where we sat shoulder to shoulder,
             crickets singing the loveliest of lullabies.
       We didn't know that there could be fulfillment in joy;
                In the moments of pure elation,
                     when the crowds fade
    and two souls dance to the music only they can hear.
  We didn't know that we didn't have to stand with bated breath,
    waiting, in anticipation for the flames of passion to implode.
  We didn't know just how much the past would affect our choices.

                                                      We didn't know...

Somewhere, along the way, we deceived ourselves
into thinking that chaos was equivalent to love.
We fooled ourselves into believing that fairytales couldn't exist,
and peace was a figment of our imagination.
We were so high on the anticipation of the unknown; the idea of
passionate destruction-
We were so sure that happiness was in our imagination,
and we weren't authors of our own story.

                                                      We were so sure...

So-

We waited, and waited for the other shoe to drop;
not realizing we were sabotaging everything we held dear.

                        We kept waiting for the end.

# THE JESTER

Laugh when you're happy,
Smile when you're sad;
Don't let the audience know when you're mad.
Dance when you're angry,
Sing through the bad;
you'll get a standing ovation,
from those blind to what they have.

Tin Man
# ISOLATION

A gray mist that doesn't go away,
A black swirl that never stops.

        The vastness of space that keeps going;
        The huge desert that no one can go through-

                A one way train ticket.

                A needle in a haystack;
                Gold at the end of a rainbow.

        The only thing that makes me cry-

Lonliness.

# IN MADNESS

Tin Man
# THE CREATION

I am not your greatest creation –
                    Or even the second greatest.

You pat my head to pacify my desire to be seen by you;
your eyes sweep over me to the male child next to me.
You nod your head in feigned appreciation at the chubby girl-hands tightly holding wilting flowers.

                                        (A plea for attention).

But the acid from your lips,
and the destruction in your hands have told me all I need to know.

                                        (I am not enough.)

Little Maker, what must your creation do to be loved by you?
What must I do to capture your attention?
When will you listen to the score of my heart? When will you see that my symphony has become a requiem?

                                (A desperate need for attention.)

Do not be alarmed when I extend my rage-filled vengeance, the vessel of retribution, on the very thing that makes you smile.

                      (If you will not accept my being, I will destroy it all.)

# CHAOS BREW

How little did you know,
that you never saw chaos brimming
right beneath the surface?

There were times when I was sure
you saw the lid ready to burst –
                            tape worn off.

But you did not help –

                            no.

Instead, you looked at me and taped the lid shut, tight.

                I am a kettle ready to shout;
          yet you placed your hand over my mouth.
            I needed someone to hear me out,
      before the rage in me spilled out of my spout.

Tin Man
# THE MONSTER

You said, the Monsters we feared lived under our beds.

        But that's a lie:
    the monsters really live inside our heads.

                      Silent.
Waiting for us to drop our guards;

                     Hiding
           amongst the refuse yard.

        When will we be free from ourselves?
        When will we stop being so overwhelmed?
    Our thoughts, our emotions, our constant prison;
        daily, haunting isolation our sole tradition.

# THE FAVORITE

"You're my favorite."

Those were the first words you said to me -
steady and calm;
a balm on an injured heart,
seeking assurance amidst daunting tides-turned-waves
ever increasing in size.

"You're my favorite."

I clung to every syllable,
every intonation of the words
as they softly fell from your mouth -
sticky and sweet like honey.
I am trapped.

"You're my favorite."

I remember.
The way those words dripped from your lips and fell on my tongue -
I savored every one.

"You were my favorite."

Those words - dark and murky -
linger still on a heart now calloused;

How painful it is to be the favorite of a heart who has other options.

# Tin Man

# STOIC

></br>If you look up stoic
>in the dictionary,
>you will find my name
>handwritten next to the definition.

The handwriting
so unfamiliar
is haphazardly scrawled out -
even trampled over other letters
just to have my name there.

Every time I open the book,
I'm reminded;
"I am strong, I am emotionless.
I will not care if I'm treated badly...
I am stoic."
My name is Stoic.

>Like a prayer, you call
>my name- whispered and sure -
>pushing me to endure
>until I am no longer my own name.
>You want Stoic.

Tin Man

"Stoic, you don't mind if I-"
"You're fine aren't you, Stoic?"
"She never has a problem. She's Stoic."
"She's Stoic. She won't care."

                                        If you look up stoic
                                              in the dictionary,
                                         you will find my name
                       handwritten next to the definition.

But        I        do        not        want        it        there.

I have tried to erase my name
many times -
black smudges where
white paper was -
yet every time I look,
my name is hastily scribbled there...
                                again.

                Like a curse, you write
              my name- loping and dark-
            Knowing that I want no part
      of the story you're writing for me.
      But my lips have been sewn shut
          with every stroke of your pen.

"Stoic,"
        you write;

Until the

e      m      o      t      i      o      n      s

        that caused the smudges on the page,
           only aid in writing the
                    same
                        story.

Tin Man
# POTENTIAL OF A ROSE

I had hoped you'd be the single rose
                         in my graveyard of bones –

                 resilient and sure;
        a symbol of hope and splendor.

Yet you have chosen to be the sickly vines
         that weave 'round my feeble femur –
Shackling me to the ever present simmer of darkness;
clinging to me as a second skin.

The potential of a rose is a facade most deadly,
                 I've learned;

                             when the potential never blossoms.

# SECRET

She whispered her secrets –
                                      hurriedly, desperately –
across the keys,
hoping that they would be kept forever.

Little did she know
her secrets, once hers –
                        now shared with the black void –
would take on a life of their own.

                          Who owns a secret with a deadly aim?
                              The victim or the keeper?

Tin Man
# OVERTONE

What am I trying to say
When the melody
Always seems to escape me
What should my hands do
When the notes run dry
Should I let my conscience die?

The words on the tip of my tongue
Won't smooth out the wrongs I've done
The notes still humming
Won't fit with the harmony
And I'm coming undone

> Tell me how do the notes resolve
> Will the dissonance last long?
> I hear the words you said echoing
> Like a cannon they surround me

> Tell me where resolution lies
> Where does the cadence die?
> Or will I be forced
> To repeat the score of my heart

Tell me what you're trying to say
Can you even hear the melody?
Fit in a sweetly sung harmony?
Truly are you listening at all
You're missing your mark
You've missed where you should start

Tell me how do the notes resolve
Will the dissonance last long?
I hear the words you said echoing
Like a cannon they surround me

Tell me where resolution lies
Where does the cadence die?
Or will I be forced
To repeat the score of my heart

Tell me where resolution lies
Where does the cadence die?

Tin Man
# STAY

> It's funny when the music dies down
> my mind, it makes the loudest sounds;
> and even if I scream and shout,
> it will never drown it out.

But if I can't hear the melodies-
echoing sweetly-
like a warming symphony;
freely embracing.
I'll likely never feel complete-
without you holding me tightly .
So sing me one more harmony,
I'm patiently waiting.

> It's funny how love's the first thing to go
> even when it's you I've called home;
> now all I can do is scream and shout,
> but your heart'd already shut me out.

But why can't I hear the melody?
Is it still echoing sweetly?
It was a warming symphony -
freely embracing.
I'll likely never feel complete-
without you holding me tightly.
Please, sing me one more symphony;
I'm still patiently waiting.

# IN SILENCE

Silence
-

I just want some silence
Is that too much to ask?
But now I hear your voice in my head
Over and over and over again
And now I need something to take off the edge
Just so I can rest

Quiet
-

Can you give me some quiet?
I'm drowning in your expectations
I've worked so hard
And burned myself out
What more could you possibly want?
Please let me be free of anxiety

But the further I push
The louder the noise
And I can't seem to hear my own voice
It's like I'm losing my way
With every breath I take
Now I can barely breathe

(The noise is deafening to me)

Tin Man
# THE MADNESS: AN OBSESSION

I know you, your greatest fears;
I see it on your face don't hold back your tears.
I know it's hard, but you're too far- gone;
the obsession I gave you has become your greatest flaw.
I know, your deepest desires;
you can't fool me, soon I'll be all that matters.

                      I know you, your deepest regrets;
                    I've pushed them away, you're in my debt.
        I know it's hard, but your back's against the wall;
                        your obsession will be your downfall.
                          I know, you've tried to run away;
                            but I don't let go so easily, Babe.

            I call -
            to you
        now I'm waiting
             -
           for you
To respond to me it's ecstasy
you see that void you feel inside
  just let me fill it for tonight

(There's nothing else I want)
                                        (No, there's nothing else I need).

      Let the delirium flow through your veins-
          until nothing else remains.

# OPHELIA'S LAMENT

I'm trying not to let it get to me,
      but I hear your words even in my sleep.
It's a never ending constant dripping;
      slowing eating at my sanity.

And even when you told me I should
-
      flee
that I should just
      leave you be;
I couldn't stop my own
-
curiosity.
      (How can I stop my own heartbeat?)
I just wanted you to want me.

I should have never given you the key–
now my heart's in need of mending;
but how do I survive the insanity
      of losing the other half of me?

Tin Man
# LIES

He's telling me lies

                                                                      (lies)

He likes my insanity
Says it's his remedy
He likes when we fight

                                                                       (fight)

Says he wants a sweeter makeup
So we should just breakup
He'll stay out all night

                                                                       (night)

He loves makin' me worry
Just so he can say "I'm sorry"
He loves to tell me lies

                                                                      (lies)

(I'm tired of his lies)

Tin Man

# IN FREEDOM

Tin Man
# SCARECROW

You laugh as I try to claw myself
out of the pit you threw me in-
                        Cackling,
                                  Gloating.
Like crows, you loudly gawk
at the scars and scabs littering my arms;
Like vultures, you circle around me-
preying I will lay down and die.

                    But I will not.

                                      I am bruised.
                                      I am scarred.
                          I am battling for peace.
                       But I will not stay here.

           I will not let you pick at the straw
             that weaves my skin and marrow.
        I will not let you pull apart the seams
        I have so desperately sewn together-
                  I will not break.

Labored breath by labored breath,
                        Inch by inch-
I will weave a new thread.

# MY JOY WAS BURIED

My joy was buried in the grave of Regret -
Half dead, forgotten;
Whispering a strained staccato chant.
Longing to see the sun again.

                          My joy was buried in the grave of Solitude -
                                          Stoic and anxious;
                            Frantically clawing at muddied memories.
                            Labored breaths, a plea for salvation.

My joy was buried in Sorrow's embrace -
Constant, steady, secure;
Promises of sweet torture and eternal misery.
Listlessly haunting vacant halls, pleading for company.

My joy was buried with-
My joy was buried-
My joy was-
My joy-

                                    Joy.

# Tin Man

The slightest sliver of light peeking through shuttered coffins,
caressing skin with warmth,
breathing life back into shriveled lungs...

                          Inhale.
                                Exhale.

The faintest breaths begin their tumultuous cycle –

                                                Inhale.
                                                          Exhale.

Slowly relearning how to live –
deep breaths, shaky hands reach outward
pushing against a tightly wound cage.

                                                Inhale.
                                       Exhale.

The faintest whisper of forgotten memories
pushing aganist tightly locked gates,
rattling the chains of apathy.

                          Hope.

Bursting forth from once desolate caverns,
a vessel once again being filled with fiery passion –
                          content, complete.

My joy was buried in the grave of Despair;
until life was breathed into Hope,
promising a new day.

# A MOMENT

Do not mistake my silence for weakness;
my meekness for apathy –
for I wish to make the most
of this fleeting moment I am given.

Though they make silence a goal,
and meekness a virtue;
I will not sit idly as fleeting moments race by.
With all the nerve I have in me,
I will awaken the young lion within–
I will build my courage.

Tin Man
# HOPE IN A WASTELAND

Here, in this wasteland
I watch my mistakes on repeat;
stuck in a place where
my memories suffocate me.

But somewhere along the way
you called out to me-
outstretched your hand;
which quieted the doubts in me.

# BEAUTY REBORN

You call her beauty;
The woman your mind remembers –
Youthful and vivacious.
She owns the very tendrils of your thoughts,
Hiding amidst the shadows of your heart –
Covered in cobwebs, lying among the refuse.
In your youth you promised her forever;
Wholeheartedly believing your love would mature with time...

All you have to show for it is ash.

Time swept in like an unforgiving current,
Carrying away all that you love;
Decaying the very essence of your heart.

                        I do not want that for us.

You admire me as you would a well-crafted Portrait;
A priceless piece of art to be displayed in your home–
Passed down from generation to generation.

You've discovered a wealth in me,
a timelessness I had never anticipated.
You handle me with a reverence I hadn't previously encountered;
Ever so delicately brushing off the dirt and mire of time,
Repairing the damaged edges.

                      For that, I thank you.

# Tin Man

# AN ARIA

Write me a song
my soul understands.
An aria that resonates so innately
I can't tell the end from the beginning.

I want to feel the words drip from your lips,
the notes dance across my tongue.
I need to feel the harmony
fold me in its arms-
envelope my very being.
So that when those dissonant chords,
those uncomfortable half steps, emerge;

I will not falter...

Because my soul knows-
soon the resolution comes.
Soon all that's gone wrong,
every piece that refused to fit-
Suddenly finds its place.

Tin Man

# A THOUSAND

a thousand prayers
before I go
-
to sleep
a thousand miles
have become
-
suffocating

when all is said and done
and i no longer feel the sun
remind me again
how you love me by
-
ten thousand

a thousand whispers
through our darkest
-
nights
a thousand moments
shouted from the highest
-
heights

when all is said and done
and we've had a good run
just remind me again
how you love me by
-
ten thousand

when I close my eyes
you are there
all through the
highs and lows
-
you've been there
when doubt
got the best of me
you, instead, loved
every inch of me

Please
when all is said and done
and our twilight years have
-
come
let me know once again
don't let me forget what you've
-
said
how you loved me by
-
ten thousand

Tin Man
# HOPE

One day (if ever) you may find yourself faced with a decision:
Live to die or die to live.
Please do not let it be the latter.
The latter means you have regrets, many things left undone,
Many places left unexplored,
Many lives left untouched.
If you- for whatever reason-
Reach this point, it's not too late.
You still have a moment,
An opportunity,
A chance to make your latter days better.

Don't give up hope.

# JOY

I hope that you live long enough to realize
the opposite of joy isn't sorrow.
In fact, I'd argue that the opposite of joy is indifference;
It's in indifference that we lose ourselves...
We lose hope.

Tin Man

# A BIRD

I was like a bird- free and wild.
The sky my only home,
the earth, my anchor
the wind, my compass
-
what a joyful sight.

You were like a cage-
cramped and suffocating.
steel arms encapsulating,
rigid in your demands
-
what an unfortunate life.

My limbs stilted and stiff
from an ill-fitting cage;
until an open window provides an escape.

Young bird, fly-
break free of the chains
weighing you down;
leave behind the worries
that trouble you.

Young bird, soar-
go to heights you'd
only dreamed of;
forsake the negative
thoughts plaguing you.

Fly, Little Bird, fly.

Tin Man
# LIONHEART

I have heard your sorrow, little heart –
seeping out through boarded windows,
I have heard the whimpers your lips have let leak.

I have seen your bruises, little heart –
battered from the constant beating down of your dreams,
never quite ceasing its assault.

I have felt your tears, little heart –
bitter rivers dropped on shaking hands,
a small refuge to troubled senses.

Little heart,
I know you suffer in silence;
continually wishing for an ear to
listen to the troubled tides stirring within you.

Little heart,
I know your hands shake as you
try to pull yourself together,
only hoping for a shoulder to lean on.

I know your pain, little heart.
I know that you are worn out from fighting with yourself;
I know that you feel weak right now.
I know that you can't see how you will manage to carry on...

But you are strong, Lionheart.

Your roar may only be
a mere mewl at the moment,
but with each shaky step
you will become stronger.
With each push forward,
you will become more powerful.

Do not grow weary, Lionheart.
Soon, you will run with
a swiftness you never thought possible;
soon, you will roar with
a ferociousness that even suprises you.
Your worries will cower away
when you walk,
your anxieties will melt
in the wake of your powerful gait-
head held high.
Take courage, Lionheart.

You will look back and smile
as you realize just how far you have walked-
just how strong you have become.
You will realize that all the storms
you have weathered
have molded the very fibers of your being.

                        Stay strong, Lionheart.

Tin Man

A film professional by day, an author and musician by night, Aurielle Chelayne received her bachelor of science in film and electronic media from Towson University. As a Maryland native, Aurielle is a lover of seafood (almost a requirement), beaches, and travel. Never one to have nothing to do, Aurielle is working on new fantasy novel series and her next collection of poetry and prose (plus, a new film script).

If you want to keep up to date with Aurielle Chelayne's next book, film, or artistic endeavor, please visit her website at http://www.auriellechelayne.com, or follow her on instagram @auriellechelayne.

Tin Man

Thank you to J Marcus for providing the amazing illustrations in this book. If you're interested in more of his illustrations, you can follow him on IG @truemarcb.

Tin Man

www.ingramcontent.com/pod-product-compliance
Lightning Source LLC
Chambersburg PA
CBHW051550010526
44118CB00022B/2653